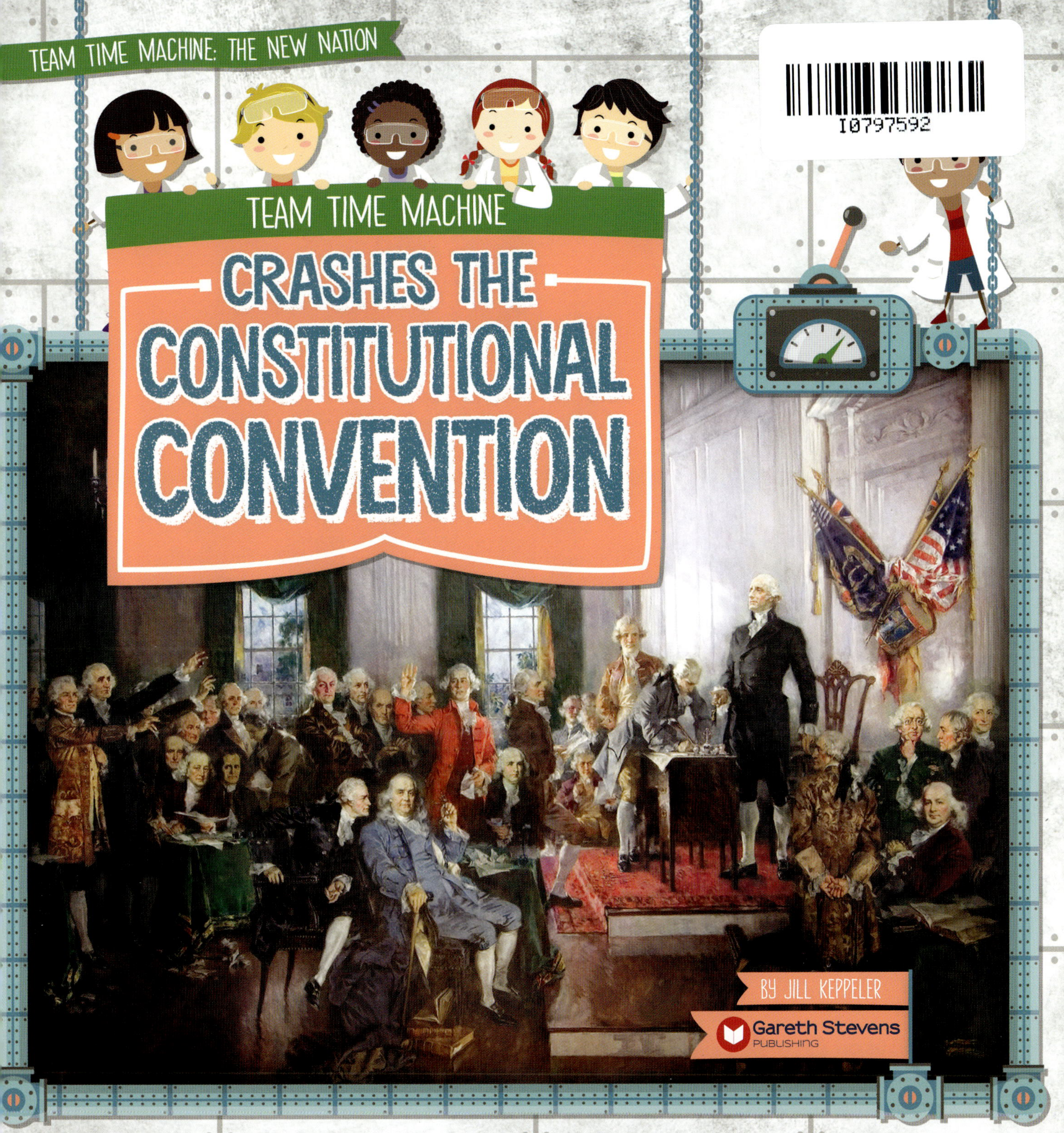
TEAM TIME MACHINE: THE NEW NATION
I0797592
TEAM TIME MACHINE
CRASHES THE
CONSTITUTIONAL
CONVENTION
BY JILL KEPPELER
Gareth Stevens
PUBLISHING

**Please visit our website, www.garethstevens.com. For a free color catalog of all our high-quality books, call toll free 1-800-542-2595 or fax 1-877-542-2596.**

**Library of Congress Cataloging-in-Publication Data**

Names: Keppeler, Jill, author.
Title: Team time machine crashes the Constitutional Convention / Jill Keppeler.
Description: New York : Gareth Stevens Publishing, 2021. | Series: Team time machine: the new nation | Includes index.
Identifiers: LCCN 2019060176 | ISBN 9781538256978 (library binding) | ISBN 9781538256954 (paperback) | ISBN 9781538256961 (6 Pack) | ISBN 9781538256985 (ebook)
Subjects: LCSH: United States. Constitutional Convention (1787)–Juvenile literature. | Constitutional history–United States–18th century Juvenile literature.
Classification: LCC KF4510 . K47 2020 | DDC 342.7302/92–dc23
LC record available at https://lccn.loc.gov/2019060176

First Edition

Published in 2021 by
**Gareth Stevens Publishing**
111 East 14th Street, Suite 349
New York, NY 10003



Designer: Katelyn E. Reynolds
Editor: Therese Shea

Photo credits: Cover, p. 1 Architect of the Capitol; cover, pp. 1–24 (series characters) Lorelyn Medina/Shutterstock.com; cover, pp. 1–24 (time machine elements) Agor2012/Shutterstock.com; cover, pp. 1–24 (background texture) somen/Shutterstock.com; p. 5 DeAgostini/Getty Images; p. 7 Festa/Shutterstock.com; p. 9 Gonzalo Azumendi/Photolibrary / Getty Images Plus; p. 11 Smith Collection/Gado/Getty Images; p. 13 (main) BoringHistoryGuy/Wikipedia.org; p. 13 (inset) John Greim/LightRocket via Getty Images; p. 15 Education Images/Universal Images Group via Getty Images; p. 17 Hulton Archive/Getty Images; p. 19 (Washington, Franklin, and Madison) Everett - Art/Shutterstock.com; p. 19 (Hamilton) Francis G. Mayer/Corbis/VCG via Getty Images; pp. 19 (Ellsworth), 23 (main) Stock Montage/Getty Images; pp. 19 (Mason), 21 (main), 29 Bettmann/Getty Images; pp. 21 (inset), 27 (inset) GraphicaArtis/Getty Images; p. 23 (inset) Andrey_Kuzmin/Shutterstock.com; p. 25 Win McNamee/Getty Images; p. 27 (main) Joseph Sohm/Shutterstock.com.



Printed in the United States of America

Some of the images in this book illustrate individuals who are models. The depictions do not imply actual situations or events.

CPSIA compliance information: Batch #CS20GS: For further information contact Gareth Stevens, New York, New York at 1-800-542-2595.

# CONTENTS



WORDS IN THE GLOSSARY APPEAR IN **BOLD** TYPE THE FIRST TIME THEY ARE USED IN THE TEXT.

# CHAPTER 1: THE PROBLEM WITH GROUPS

"Wait!" yelled Gaby. "Is something wrong, Zoe?"

Zoe had run out of science club when it ended. Gaby and Will raced to catch up with her. Zoe stopped and turned around. She looked upset.

"It's this group project," she told them. "I really wish I was in your group. In mine, nobody can agree on anything. Some people aren't even showing up!"

Will gave her an understanding look. "It will be okay," he said. "Remember what we learned about the Constitutional Convention?"

## MEET TEAM TIME MACHINE

TEAM TIME MACHINE IS A GROUP OF FRIENDS WHO FOUND A TIME MACHINE ONE DAY IN A VERY ODD LIBRARY. THEY DISCOVERED THAT BOOKS FROM THE LIBRARY COULD POWER THE MACHINE AND TRANSPORT THEM TO DIFFERENT PLACES AND TIMES. IN THIS ADVENTURE, GABY, ZOE, AND WILL VISIT THE CONSTITUTIONAL CONVENTION IN PHILADELPHIA, PENNSYLVANIA!

SOME **FOUNDING FATHERS** WERE MISSING FROM THE CONSTITUTIONAL CONVENTION OF 1787. FOR EXAMPLE, PATRICK HENRY REFUSED TO GO. HE FEARED IT WOULD CREATE A NATIONAL GOVERNMENT THAT WAS TOO POWERFUL.

Zoe gave Will a puzzled look. "Constitutional Convention? Do you mean that meeting in 1787 that created the Constitution? What does science club have to do with that?"

Gaby snapped her fingers. "Will's right. There were all kinds of problems during it. **Delegates** were late or didn't show up at all. Nobody agreed on anything. An entire state wouldn't take part!"

Will nodded. "But they got the job done," he added. "Let's use the time machine to see how they did it!"

Zoe perked up. "To the library!" she said.

THE U.S. CONSTITUTION IS THE OLDEST WRITTEN CONSTITUTION STILL IN USE BY A COUNTRY. A CONSTITUTION IS THE BASIC LAWS OF A NATION.

# CHAPTER 2: THE TEAM IN PHILADELPHIA

There were a few books on the Constitutional Convention in the library. Zoe picked one and put it in the time machine. Then she nodded to the others and pulled the handle. The room spun!

The kids held on to the shelves and waited until the room stopped. Gaby went to the door and looked out.

"Looks like early Philadelphia!" she called back to her friends. "We're here!"

Will nodded, checking the machine. "May 25, 1787," he said. "Perfect."

THE CONSTITUTIONAL CONVENTION OPENED MAY 14, 1787—BUT DELEGATES FROM ONLY TWO STATES WERE THERE! ON MAY 25, THERE WERE FINALLY ENOUGH DELEGATES TO START.

EVEN TODAY, SOME PARTS OF PHILADELPHIA LOOK MUCH LIKE THEY DID YEARS AGO. THESE HOUSES ARE ON ELFRETH'S ALLEY, THE OLDEST **RESIDENTIAL** STREET IN THE UNITED STATES.

The kids stepped out of the library. From the outside, it looked like the brick buildings around it.

"Okay, to the Pennsylvania State House, team!" said Zoe. She had taken a look at another book in the library and learned that's where the delegates to the Constitutional Convention had met.

The team stopped to talk to some boys playing nearby. Will traded some candy he had for directions.

"Good thing I had chocolate with me," Will smiled.

Gaby laughed, "Will, you always have chocolate!"

PHILADELPHIA WAS AN IMPORTANT CITY IN THE EARLY UNITED STATES. HERE IS AN ARTIST'S IDEA OF WHAT IT LOOKED LIKE IN THE EARLY 1800s.

# CHAPTER 3: THE STATE HOUSE

It didn't take long for the kids to find the tall building called the Pennsylvania State House. The state's government met there. In fact, the Continental Congress, the delegates of the American colonies, had met there before and during the **American Revolution**. They approved the Declaration of Independence there in 1776.

The kids quietly followed men walking into the building.

"This is so exciting!" Gaby whispered.

Zoe looked around. "Yeah, but . . . a lot of these people don't look too happy."

BY MAY 25, 1787, DELEGATES FROM SEVEN STATES HAD ARRIVED AT THE CONSTITUTIONAL CONVENTION. OTHERS ARRIVED LATER.

THE PENNSYLVANIA STATE HOUSE, SHOWN HERE IN 1799, IS NOW CALLED INDEPENDENCE HALL.

# CHAPTER 4: IT'S A SECRET!

Standing in the back of the hall, the kids watched as the delegates took their seats. They knew they had to stay quiet and not call attention to themselves. The delegates had agreed that their meetings would stay completely secret from outsiders.

Even the doors and windows were shut tight. It was very hot and crowded in the room. Will pulled at his collar and sighed.

"I wish they had **air-conditioning** in 1787," he whispered. "This is going to be rough!"

WE KNEW WHAT HAPPENED AT THE CONSTITUTIONAL CONVENTION BECAUSE DELEGATES, LIKE JAMES MADISON, TOOK NOTES.

DELEGATES MET IN THE ASSEMBLY ROOM IN INDEPENDENCE HALL. YOU DON'T NEED A TIME MACHINE TO VISIT IT—IT'S STILL THERE!

# CHAPTER 5: ARGUING ABOUT THE ARTICLES

First, the delegates agreed that George Washington should be president of the convention. They began talking about why they were there. They were worried about the new nation. There were many problems under its first constitution, called the Articles of Confederation. The federal, or national, government wasn't strong enough to hold the states together. It couldn't solve arguments between states. It had no money and a lot of **debt**.

Some delegates wanted to **amend** the Articles. Others, like James Madison and Alexander Hamilton, talked about creating a new constitution.

THE DELEGATES CHOSE THREE MEN, INCLUDING ALEXANDER HAMILTON, TO COME UP WITH RULES FOR THE CONVENTION.

GEORGE WASHINGTON WAS THE GENERAL OF THE COLONIAL AND U.S. ARMIES FROM 1775 TO 1783. IN 1789, AFTER THE CONSTITUTIONAL CONVENTION, HE BECAME THE FIRST PRESIDENT OF THE UNITED STATES.

As the meeting ended for the day, Zoe looked at Will and Gaby. "You were right!" she said. "They're already arguing about things."

Gaby frowned. "They don't sign the Constitution until September," she said. "It's only May. There will be a lot more arguments! We can't stay that long."

Will nodded. "There will be more delegates next week," he remembered. "And that's when they'll agree—mostly—on coming up with a new constitution. Let's come back then."

Time was no problem for Team Time Machine!

THE STATES CHOSE 74 DELEGATES TO ATTEND THE CONVENTION. ONLY 55 WENT. NO MORE THAN 30 STAYED THE WHOLE TIME.

## FAMOUS DELEGATES TO THE CONSTITUTIONAL CONVENTION

GEORGE WASHINGTON (VIRGINIA)

BENJAMIN FRANKLIN (PENNSYLVANIA)

JAMES MADISON (VIRGINIA)

ALEXANDER HAMILTON (NEW YORK)

OLIVER ELLSWORTH (CONNECTICUT)

GEORGE MASON (VIRGINIA)

# CHAPTER 6: A NEW CONSTITUTION

On May 30, 1787, Gaby, Will, and Zoe were back at the state house. They stood quietly in their corner and listened. The day before, Virginia delegate Edmund Randolph had talked about the problems with the Articles of Confederation and offered a plan for a new government. Everyone called it the Virginia Plan. Another Virginia delegate, future president James Madison, had written it.

"And just like that," Gaby said, "there will be a new constitution!"

Zoe shook her head. "It won't be that easy."

ONE MAJOR PART OF THE VIRGINIA PLAN WAS A FEDERAL GOVERNMENT DIVIDED INTO THREE SEPARATE BRANCHES WITH EQUAL POWER.

WHEN WASHINGTON BECAME PRESIDENT, HE ASKED SOME MEN WHO HAD BEEN DELEGATES TO THE CONVENTION TO JOIN HIS CABINET (BELOW). THE CABINET IS A GROUP OF ADVISORS TO THE PRESIDENT.
ALEXANDER HAMILTON
HENRY KNOX
GEORGE WASHINGTON
THOMAS JEFFERSON
EDMUND RANDOLPH
JAMES MADISON

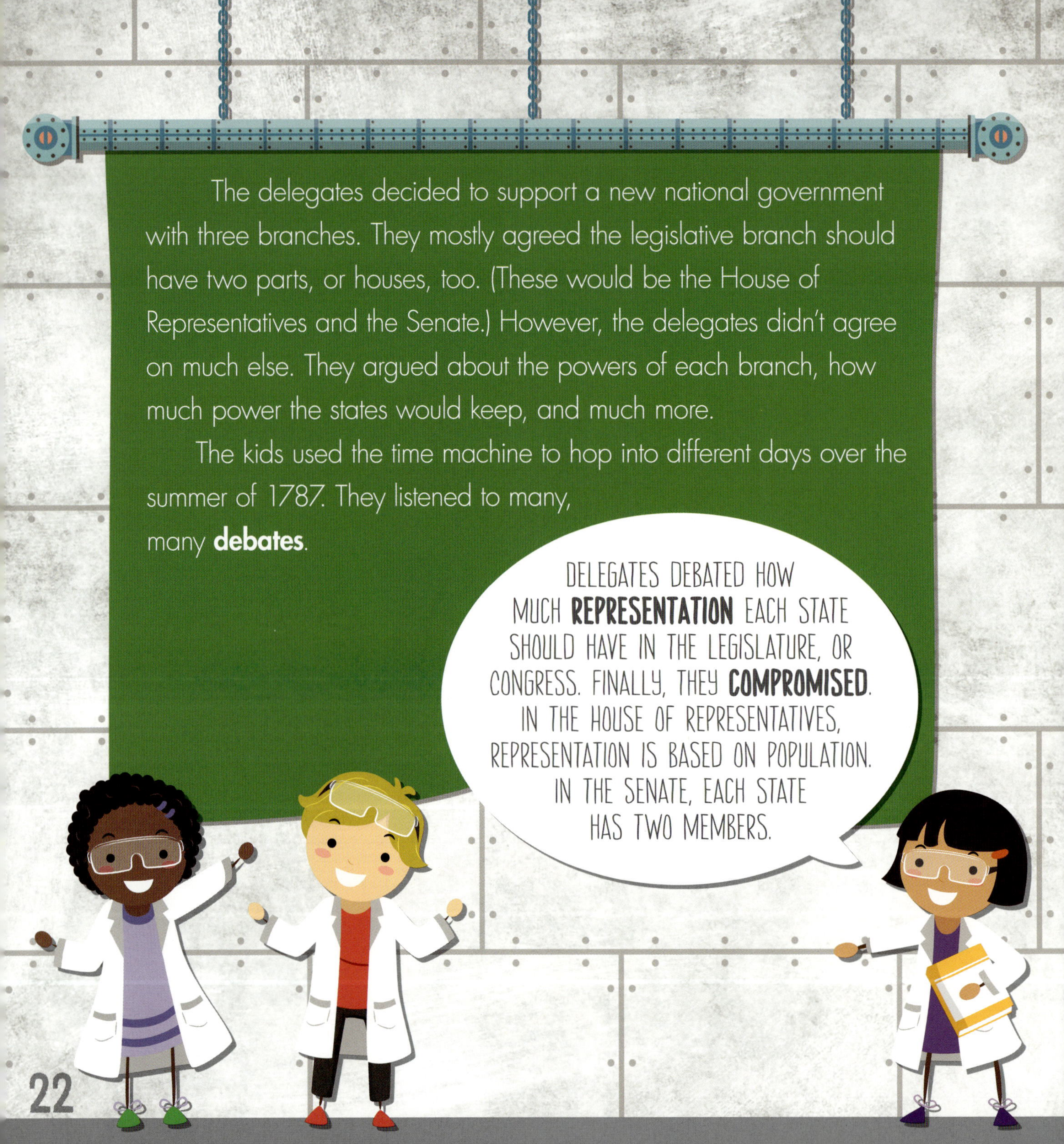

The delegates decided to support a new national government with three branches. They mostly agreed the legislative branch should have two parts, or houses, too. (These would be the House of Representatives and the Senate.) However, the delegates didn't agree on much else. They argued about the powers of each branch, how much power the states would keep, and much more.

The kids used the time machine to hop into different days over the summer of 1787. They listened to many, many **debates**.

BY JULY 24, 1787, ALL THE DETAILS, OR PARTS, OF THE NEW GOVERNMENT HADN'T BEEN DECIDED YET. STILL, THE DELEGATES CHOSE A **COMMITTEE** OF DETAIL TO WRITE UP THE NEW CONSTITUTION. JOHN RUTLEDGE, SHOWN, WAS THE COMMITTEE'S HEAD.

## THE THREE BRANCHES OF THE U.S. GOVERNMENT

**LEGISLATIVE BRANCH:**
MAKES THE LAWS (CONGRESS)

**EXECUTIVE BRANCH:**
CARRIES OUT THE LAWS (PRESIDENT)

**JUDICIAL BRANCH:**
EXPLAINS THE LAWS (FEDERAL COURTS)

# CHAPTER 7: TAKING NOTES, MAKING CHANGES

The Constitutional Convention didn't meet while the Committee of Detail worked. On August 6, 1787, Zoe, Gaby, and Will came back when the convention started to debate the committee's constitution.

"Great," Will sighed. "More arguing."

Gaby hid a smile and said, "Everyone has different concerns and ideas. They have to decide what compromises they're willing to make to get what they want most."

"The delegates knew how important the convention was," said Zoe. "Just think, we're still using the U.S. Constitution more than 200 years later."

SOME DELEGATES CAME AND WENT OVER THE FOUR MONTHS OF THE CONSTITUTIONAL CONVENTION. NEW HAMPSHIRE'S DELEGATES DIDN'T ARRIVE UNTIL JULY!

THIS IS GEORGE WASHINGTON'S MARKED-UP COPY OF AN EARLY U.S. CONSTITUTION. AFTER THE CONVENTION DEBATED IT, THEY NAMED A COMMITTEE OF STYLE TO FIX THE WORDING.

[ 5 ]

Stricken out

or cauſe, the court ſhall nevertheleſs proceed to
judgment ſhall be final and concluſive. The pr
to the Preſident of the Senate, and ſhall be lodg
for the ſecurity of the parties concerned. Every
ſit in judgment, take an oath, to be adminiſtere
ſupreme or ſuperior court of the State where th
" and truly to hear and determine the matter i
" beſt of his judgment, without favour, affectio

Stricken out.

*Sect.* 3. All controverſies concerning lands c
of two or more States, whoſe juriſdictions, as
have been decided or adjuſted ſubſequent to ſuch
on application to the Senate, be finally determin
ſame manner as is before preſcribed for deciding
ent States.

X.

*Sect.* 1. The Executive Power of the United
gle perſon. His ſtile ſhall be, " The Preſident
" ca;" and his title ſhall be, " His Excellen
ballot by the Legiſlature.+ He ſhall hold his off
years; but ſhall not be elected a ſecond time.

which election a majority
votes of the members present
be required

*Sect.* 2. He ſhall, from time to time, give inf
the State of the Union: ~~he may~~ and recommend to
ſures as he ſhall judge neceſſary, and expedient:
traordinary occaſions. and In caſe of diſagreement
regard to the time of adjournment, he may a

# CHAPTER 8: SIGNED!

After so much hopping through time, Team Time Machine made sure they were there on September 17, 1787. They watched and listened as the U.S. Constitution was read aloud. They grinned at each other as delegates signed it.

But three men—Elbridge Gerry, Edmund Randolph, and George Mason—wouldn't sign it. Zoe frowned. "After all that work!" she said.

"But enough delegates will sign," Gaby said. "And by next year, enough states will approve it to make it law. Then, the **Bill of Rights** will be added in 1791."

ELBRIDGE GERRY, EDMUND RANDOLPH, AND GEORGE MASON WOULDN'T SIGN THE CONSTITUTION BECAUSE THEY WANTED A BILL OF RIGHTS TO GUARD THE RIGHTS OF THE STATES AND THE PEOPLE. THESE ARE THE FIRST 10 **AMENDMENTS**.

BENJAMIN FRANKLIN SAID HE HAD OFTEN LOOKED AT WASHINGTON'S CHAIR AND WONDERED IF THE SUN ON IT WAS RISING OR SETTING. HE SAID HE KNEW IT WAS RISING WHEN THE CONSTITUTION WAS APPROVED BY THE CONVENTION.

BENJAMIN FRANKLIN

# CHAPTER 9: ALL'S WELL THAT ENDS WELL

Zoe skipped down the street as they headed back to the library. "I can't believe all that arguing ended with the U.S. Constitution!" she exclaimed. "It almost seemed like the country was going to fall apart."

Will and Gaby laughed. "It makes your science project group look better, doesn't it?" Gaby asked as they reached the library.

Zoe made a face. "A bit," she said as they slipped in the door. "Maybe my group can stop the arguing and make some compromises too!"

SOME SIGNERS OF THE CONSTITUTION WORKED HARD AFTER THE CONVENTION TO GET THE STATES TO RATIFY, OR APPROVE, IT. IN TIME, ALL DID.

# GLOSSARY

**air-conditioning:** a system used for cooling and drying air

**amend:** to change or add something to a piece of writing

**amendment:** a change or addition to a constitution

**American Revolution:** the war in which the colonies won their freedom from England

**Bill of Rights:** a written statement that lists the basic rights of the citizens of a country

**committee:** a group of people chosen to do a certain job

**compromise:** reaching an agreement in which each side gives up something to end an argument

**debate:** an argument or public discussion. Also, to have an argument or public discussion.

**debt:** an amount of money owed

**delegate:** a representative of one of the 13 colonies

**Founding Father:** a man who had an important part in creating the government of the United States

**representation:** a person or group of people who speak or act for others

**residential:** having mostly homes instead of businesses

# FOR MORE INFORMATION

## BOOKS

Demuth, Patricia Brennan. *What Is the Constitution?* New York, NY: Penguin Workshop, 2018.

Khan, Khizr. *This Is Our Constitution: Discover America with a Gold Star Father.* New York, NY: Knopf, 2017.

## WEBSITES

**The Constitutional Convention**
*bensguide.gpo.gov/m-constitutional-convention*
Learn more about what happened at the convention.

**Twenty Questions Kids Ask the Most on Constitution Day**
*constitutioncenter.org/blog/20-questions-kids-ask-the-most-on-constitution-day*
Find out more about the U.S. Constitution.

**What Are Checks and Balances?**
*www.wonderopolis.org/wonder/what-are-checks-and-balances*
Discover more about the branches of government set up by the Constitution.

# INDEX